THE NATIONAL TRUST

Heritage Diary

1994

THE NATIONAL TRUST

Published in Great Britain by
The National Trust (Enterprises) Ltd, 36 Queen Anne's Gate,
London SW1H 9AS

© 1993 The National Trust

ISBN 0 7078 0174 5

COVER: Detail from a design for a nursery chintz hanging at
Wightwick Manor, West Midlands, entitled 'The House that Jack
Built' by Charles Francis Annesley Voysey, 1929. *British
Architectural Library (RIBA)*.

The National Trust would like to thank the following for their
kind permission to use material: the Estate of Charles Carrington
for *Rudyard Kipling* by Charles Carrington, Lord Egremont and
Macmillan and Company for *Wyndham and Children First*, Victor
Gollancz for the *Journal of Mary Elizabeth Lucy* from *Mistress of
Charlecote* by Alice Fairfax-Lucy, HarperCollins for *The Jealous
Governess or the Granted Wish* by Daisy and Angela Ashford,
Lennard Publishing for *Astride the Wall* by Ursula Wyndham
(1988), John Murray (Publishers) Ltd for *Christmas* from *Collected
Poems* by John Betjeman, Nigel Nicolson and Weidenfeld and
Nicolson for *Portrait of a Marriage*, and the Estate of Phyllis
Elinor Sandeman for *Treasure on Earth*.

The alphabet illustrations used as chapter openings are
reproduced from *The Oxford Nursery Rhyme Book* pp.106–7,
assembled by Iona and Peter Opie, published by Oxford University
Press (1955), by permission.

Articles by Alison Honey
Designed by Humphrey Stone

Phototypeset by Southern Positives and Negatives (SPAN),
Lingfield, Surrey (8944)
Printed by
South Sea International Press Ltd, Hong Kong

Contents

1994

	JANUARY
Monday	3 10 17 24 31
Tuesday	4 11 18 25
Wednesday	5 12 19 26
Thursday	6 13 20 27
Friday	7 14 21 28
Saturday	1 8 15 22 29
Sunday	2 9 16 23 30

	FEBRUARY
Monday	7 14 21 28
Tuesday	1 8 15 22
Wednesday	2 9 16 23
Thursday	3 10 17 24
Friday	4 11 18 25
Saturday	5 12 19 26
Sunday	6 13 20 27

	MARCH
Monday	7 14 21 28
Tuesday	1 8 15 22 29
Wednesday	2 9 16 23 30
Thursday	3 10 17 24 31
Friday	4 11 18 25
Saturday	5 12 19 26
Sunday	6 13 20 27

	APRIL
Monday	4 11 18 25
Tuesday	5 12 19 26
Wednesday	6 13 20 27
Thursday	7 14 21 28
Friday	1 8 15 22 29
Saturday	2 9 16 23 30
Sunday	3 10 17 24

	MAY
Monday	2 9 16 23 30
Tuesday	3 10 17 24 31
Wednesday	4 11 18 25
Thursday	5 12 19 26
Friday	6 13 20 27
Saturday	7 14 21 28
Sunday	1 8 15 22 29

	JUNE
Monday	6 13 20 27
Tuesday	7 14 21 28
Wednesday	1 8 15 22 29
Thursday	2 9 16 23 30
Friday	3 10 17 24
Saturday	4 11 18 25
Sunday	5 12 19 26

	JULY
Monday	4 11 18 25
Tuesday	5 12 19 26
Wednesday	6 13 20 27
Thursday	7 14 21 28
Friday	1 8 15 22 29
Saturday	2 9 16 23 30
Sunday	3 10 17 24 31

	AUGUST
Monday	1 8 15 22 29
Tuesday	2 9 16 23 30
Wednesday	3 10 17 24 31
Thursday	4 11 18 25
Friday	5 12 19 26
Saturday	6 13 20 27
Sunday	7 14 21 28

	SEPTEMBER
Monday	5 12 19 26
Tuesday	6 13 20 27
Wednesday	7 14 21 28
Thursday	1 8 15 22 29
Friday	2 9 16 23 30
Saturday	3 10 17 24
Sunday	4 11 18 25

	OCTOBER
Monday	3 10 17 24 31
Tuesday	4 11 18 25
Wednesday	5 12 19 26
Thursday	6 13 20 27
Friday	7 14 21 28
Saturday	1 8 15 22 29
Sunday	2 9 16 23 30

	NOVEMBER
Monday	7 14 21 28
Tuesday	1 8 15 22 29
Wednesday	2 9 16 23 30
Thursday	3 10 17 24
Friday	4 11 18 25
Saturday	5 12 19 26
Sunday	6 13 20 27

	DECEMBER
Monday	5 12 19 26
Tuesday	6 13 20 27
Wednesday	7 14 21 28
Thursday	1 8 15 22 29
Friday	2 9 16 23 30
Saturday	3 10 17 24 31
Sunday	4 11 18 25

1993

	JANUARY				
Monday		4	11	18	25
Tuesday		5	12	19	26
Wednesday		6	13	20	27
Thursday		7	14	21	28
Friday	1	8	15	22	29
Saturday	2	9	16	23	30
Sunday	3	10	17	24	31

	FEBRUARY			
Monday	1	8	15	22
Tuesday	2	9	16	23
Wednesday	3	10	17	24
Thursday	4	11	18	25
Friday	5	12	19	26
Saturday	6	13	20	27
Sunday	7	14	21	28

	MARCH				
Monday	1	8	15	22	29
Tuesday	2	9	16	23	30
Wednesday	3	10	17	24	31
Thursday	4	11	18	25	
Friday	5	12	19	26	
Saturday	6	13	20	27	
Sunday	7	14	21	28	

	APRIL			
Monday		5	12	19	26
Tuesday		6	13	20	27
Wednesday		7	14	21	28
Thursday	1	8	15	22	29
Friday	2	9	16	23	30
Saturday	3	10	17	24	
Sunday	4	11	18	25	

	MAY				
Monday		3	10	17	24	31
Tuesday		4	11	18	25
Wednesday		5	12	19	26
Thursday		6	13	20	27
Friday		7	14	21	28
Saturday	1	8	15	22	29
Sunday	2	9	16	23	30

	JUNE			
Monday		7	14	21	28
Tuesday	1	8	15	22	29
Wednesday	2	9	16	23	30
Thursday	3	10	17	24
Friday	4	11	18	25
Saturday	5	12	19	26
Sunday	6	13	20	27

	JULY			
Monday		5	12	19	26
Tuesday		6	13	20	27
Wednesday		7	14	21	28
Thursday	1	8	15	22	29
Friday	2	9	16	23	30
Saturday	3	10	17	24	31
Sunday	4	11	18	25

	AUGUST				
Monday	2	9	16	23	30
Tuesday	3	10	17	24	31
Wednesday	4	11	18	25	
Thursday	5	12	19	26	
Friday	6	13	20	27	
Saturday	7	14	21	28	
Sunday	1	8	15	22	29

	SEPTEMBER			
Monday		6	13	20	27
Tuesday		7	14	21	28
Wednesday	1	8	15	22	29
Thursday	2	9	16	23	30
Friday	3	10	17	24
Saturday	4	11	18	25
Sunday	5	12	19	26

	OCTOBER				
Monday		4	11	18	25
Tuesday		5	12	19	26
Wednesday		6	13	20	27
Thursday		7	14	21	28
Friday	1	8	15	22	29
Saturday	2	9	16	23	30
Sunday	3	10	17	24	31

	NOVEMBER			
Monday	1	8	15	22	29
Tuesday	2	9	16	23	30
Wednesday	3	10	17	24
Thursday	4	11	18	25
Friday	5	12	19	26
Saturday	6	13	20	27
Sunday	7	14	21	28

	DECEMBER			
Monday		6	13	20	27
Tuesday		7	14	21	28
Wednesday	1	8	15	22	29
Thursday	2	9	16	23	30
Friday	3	10	17	24	31
Saturday	4	11	18	25
Sunday	5	12	19	26

1995

	JANUARY				
Monday	2	9	16	23	30
Tuesday	3	10	17	24	31
Wednesday	4	11	18	25	
Thursday	5	12	19	26	
Friday	6	13	20	27	
Saturday	7	14	21	28	
Sunday	1	8	15	22	29

	FEBRUARY			
Monday		6	13	20	27
Tuesday		7	14	21	28
Wednesday	1	8	15	22
Thursday	2	9	16	23
Friday	3	10	17	24
Saturday	4	11	18	25
Sunday	5	12	19	26

	MARCH			
Monday		6	13	20	27
Tuesday		7	14	21	28
Wednesday	1	8	15	22	29
Thursday	2	9	16	23	30
Friday	3	10	17	24	31
Saturday	4	11	18	25
Sunday	5	12	19	26

	APRIL			
Monday		3	10	17	24
Tuesday		4	11	18	25
Wednesday		5	12	19	26
Thursday		6	13	20	27
Friday		7	14	21	28
Saturday	1	8	15	22	29
Sunday	2	9	16	23	30

	MAY			
Monday	1	8	15	22	29
Tuesday	2	9	16	23	30
Wednesday	3	10	17	24	31
Thursday	4	11	18	25
Friday	5	12	19	26
Saturday	6	13	20	27
Sunday	7	14	21	28

	JUNE			
Monday		5	12	19	26
Tuesday		6	13	20	27
Wednesday		7	14	21	28
Thursday	1	8	15	22	29
Friday	2	9	16	23	30
Saturday	3	10	17	24
Sunday	4	11	18	25

	JULY				
Monday		3	10	17	24	31
Tuesday		4	11	18	25
Wednesday		5	12	19	26
Thursday		6	13	20	27
Friday		7	14	21	28
Saturday	1	8	15	22	29
Sunday	2	9	16	23	30

	AUGUST				
Monday		7	14	21	28
Tuesday	1	8	15	22	29
Wednesday	2	9	16	23	30
Thursday	3	10	17	24	31
Friday	4	11	18	25
Saturday	5	12	19	26
Sunday	6	13	20	27

	SEPTEMBER			
Monday		4	11	18	25
Tuesday		5	12	19	26
Wednesday		6	13	20	27
Thursday		7	14	21	28
Friday	1	8	15	22	29
Saturday	2	9	16	23	30
Sunday	3	10	17	24

	OCTOBER				
Monday		2	9	16	23	30
Tuesday		3	10	17	24	31
Wednesday		4	11	18	25
Thursday		5	12	19	26
Friday		6	13	20	27
Saturday		7	14	21	28
Sunday	1	8	15	22	29

	NOVEMBER			
Monday		6	13	20	27
Tuesday		7	14	21	28
Wednesday	1	8	15	22	29
Thursday	2	9	16	23	30
Friday	3	10	17	24
Saturday	4	11	18	25
Sunday	5	12	19	26

	DECEMBER			
Monday		4	11	18	25
Tuesday		5	12	19	26
Wednesday		6	13	20	27
Thursday		7	14	21	28
Friday	1	8	15	22	29
Saturday	2	9	16	23	30
Sunday	3	10	17	24	31

Samuel Sketchley, his wife and four sons. This painting by an unknown artist, c.1790, hangs in Peckover House, Cambridgeshire. (NTPL/Christopher Hurst)

Introduction

he National Trust is often seen as a venerable institution, representing maturity rather than youth – a preconception that we hope is receding. There are, in fact, many National Trust links with childhood. For instance, within several properties, memories and experiences of childhood are so strong that visitors are immediately aware of their influence. At Bateman's in East Sussex, the bell over the front door reminded Rudyard Kipling of the idyllic month he spent each year with his relatives in London – an oasis in the desert of misery that was his childhood in Southsea, far from his parents in India. The great house at Knole in Kent, inspired Vita Sackville-West, the wild and wayward tomboy who grew up there, enraptured by its romantic past.

At the Museum of Childhood at Sudbury Hall in Derbyshire, now run by the National Trust, visitors can experience for themselves through toys, games and books how children over the past two centuries have played, learnt and worked.

The articles in this diary have been written by Alison Honey, formerly the National Trust's children's editor, and author of several National Trust books for young people.

JANUARY

The Songs of Death

The Songs of Death

One evening late in Sep: Mr. Hose sat in his armchair reading a news paper. His wife sat in an other looking at the "Strand" Magerzine. Mr. Hose sudonly looked up at his wife; "Elizabeth" he said "one thing I have been wishing for, ever scince we were married is a baby, would you not like to have one looking at her seariously "Yes indeed I should" ansed his delicat wife with a sigh.

Angela Ashford *The Jealous Governes or The Granted Wish*
(written in 1893 when the author was eight years old)

he longed-for baby is safely delivered to the couple that same evening, in a cardboard box tied up with string from which 'a dear little fat little baby rolled out on to the eider down'. Angela Ashford's grasp of family planning and childbirth was about as loose as her grasp of spelling: in the real world things were not quite so simple. Before the days of reliable contraception it was quite common for women to be in a state of almost continuous pregnancy. This was particularly so amongst the upper classes where there was a vogue for farming babies out to wet nurses – breastfeeding was one of the most effective means of natural contraception. As a consequence a woman had hardly recovered from one birth before she was once again in the dangerous state of pregnancy, putting her own life, and that of her unborn baby, at risk.

Lady Elizabeth Brownlow, grandmother of 'Young' Sir John Brownlow, the builder of Belton House in Lincolnshire, bore her husband nineteen children between 1626 and 1648 but only six of these survived. Countless other examples of infant deaths and miscarriages pepper the pages of history books and records – it was one area of life which struck rich and poor alike. Perhaps one of the most tragic royal cases was the

OPPOSITE *One of a series of Victorian coloured prints entitled*
'Nursing Mothers' which hang in the day nursery at
Arlington Court, Devon. (NTPL/Derrick E. Whitty)

death of Princess Charlotte, the only child of the Prince Regent, in childbirth in 1817. She and her husband, Prince Leopold, lived at Claremont in Surrey for the eighteen months of their brief marriage. A popular couple, they had been the hope of the country at a time when King George III was mad and the Regent was drunk most of the time. However, after a traumatic labour of 52 hours the 21-year-old princess gave birth to a stillborn son; she died of a haemorrhage and shock the following morning. Having been dosed with brandy to numb the pain, her last words were said to have been 'They have made me tipsy'. The monarchy had lost two heirs in one fell swoop and the country was distraught: the tea-house at Claremont was turned into a mausoleum to Charlotte's memory; one of the potteries issued an inapt set of *nursery* china commemorating the sad event; and the royal physician, Sir Richard Croft, was so depressed at his apparent failure to save mother and son that he shot himself three months later. His descendants still live at Croft Castle in Herefordshire. Other bizarre commemorations included a wonderfully excessive painting entitled the *Apotheosis of the Royal Family* which hangs in Wimpole Hall in Cambridgeshire. It depicts Britannia mourning for the deceased members of George IV's family who float above her in heavenly splendour, including Princess Charlotte and her child perched on cotton-wool clouds.

It is not surprising that Queen Victoria referred to pregnancy and childbirth as the *Schattenseite*, or shadow side, of marriage although she appears to have sailed through nine births without miscarriage, infant death or danger to herself. In Victoria's mind childbirth was 'the ONLY thing I dread' and in fact the whole business of babies had no appeal to the young Queen – she was revolted by breastfeeding and thought that 'An ugly baby is a very nasty object, and the prettiest is frightful when undressed'. Delighted at the introduction of chloroform as a painkiller, Victoria had no compunction in using it during the birth of her eighth child, Leopold, in 1853 and described the effect as 'soothing, quieting & delightful beyond measure'. She did not, however, go to the same ecstatic lengths as one grateful mother who christened her daughter Anaesthesia as testament to her pain-free labour.

Even when babies had been delivered safely into the world there was yet another hurdle to overcome: to survive childhood. London bills of mortality for 1765 showed a 60 per cent death rate for children under two years old and in 1851 only 50 per cent of babies were expected to reach their fifth birthday. Insanitary conditions and the rapid spread of disease took much of the blame – epidemics of smallpox, measles, diphtheria and other illnesses could wipe out whole generations of

Apotheosis of the Royal Family *depicts Britannia mourning
the deceased members of George IV's family and their reunion in heaven.
The picture, painted by an unknown British artist in 1829,
hangs in Wimpole Hall, Cambridgeshire. (NTPL/Roy Fox)*

families at a time. In 1888 at Wicken Fen in Cambridgeshire, George Butcher, a peat cutter, and his wife Ellen lost three of their four children to diphtheria. Large families at least meant that statistically there was more chance of some surviving. Sir John Verney (1640–1717), master of Claydon House in Buckinghamshire, lost two of his fifteen children but was thankful that at least he had a baker's dozen left alive. Others had little choice but to take a stoical view: Sir William Brownlow who saw six of his nineteen die declared that 'though my children die, the Lord liveth and they exchange but a temporal life for an eternal one.'

In the nineteenth century medicine and improved living conditions made childbirth and childhood safer. From 1801 to 1911 the population grew by over eleven per cent per year and the average family had six or seven children. Better medical care could, ironically, result in total exhaustion for the mother – Edward Lear's mother gave birth to 22 children in the early years of the nineteenth century. They all survived and as a result Mrs Lear died relatively young from 'general decay'. It seemed that women were doomed either way.

1
Saturday

2
Sunday

'Can I, who have for others oft compiled
The songs of death, forget my sweetest child,
Which, like a flower crushed, with a blast is dead,
And ere full time hangs down his smiling head,
Expecting with clear hope to live anew
Among the angels fed with heavenly dew?'

On my dear son, Gervase, Sir John Beaumont (1582–1627)

3
Monday

BANK HOLIDAY (UK)

4
Tuesday

BANK HOLIDAY (SCOTLAND)

5
Wednesday

6
Thursday

EPIPHANY

7
Friday

8
Saturday

9
Sunday

'George used to have barrels of drinking water sent from Petworth to London as he didn't
want to risk his children catching typhoid fever from drinking London water. The
practice continued until 13 January 1895 when Uncle George died of typhoid fever
contracted at Petworth.'

Wyndham and Children First, Lord Egremont, 1968

10
Monday

11
Tuesday

12
Wednesday

13
Thursday

14
Friday

15
Saturday

16
Sunday

'There are only two things a child will share willingly – communicable diseases and his mother's age.'

Benjamin Spock (b.1903)

17
Monday

18
Tuesday

19
Wednesday

20
Thursday

21
Friday

22
Saturday

23
Sunday

'What you say of the pride of giving life to an immortal soul is very fine, dear, but I own I cannot enter into that, I think much more of our being like a cow or a dog at such moments, when our poor nature becomes so very animal and unecstatic.'

Queen Victoria writing to her eldest daughter, Princess Victoria, in 1858

24
Monday

25
Tuesday

26
Wednesday

27
Thursday

28
Friday

29
Saturday

30
Sunday

31
Monday

Mary Elizabeth Lucy endured the trauma of losing her baby, Edmund Davenport, while on the Grand Tour in 1840. On the coach journey from Lyons to Turin the child died in Mary's arms.

'Eleven long hours did I travel with his dear lifeless body on my lap ere we reached Turin at three o'clock in the morning. Never, never can I forget that night of anguish, seated in the carriage with the moon shining bright through the window on that pale but beauteous face – so calm, so still, so lovely in death.'

Mistress of Charlecote: the memoirs of Mary Elizabeth Lucy, edited by Alice Fairfax-Lucy, 1983

FEBRUARY

Sugar and Spice, Frogs
and Snails

Theresa Parker of Saltram House in Devon with her son, Jack, painted by Joshua Reynolds. Jack was only three years old when his mother died in 1775, after giving birth to a daughter. (NTPL)

Sugar and Spice, Frogs and Snails

others must give up their boys but keep girls constantly under their eye.' Theresa Parker, the eighteenth-century mistress of Saltram House in Devon, neatly summed up the difference in the treatment of each sex. Although for the first years of their lives boys and girls looked indistinguishable, dressed in petticoats and sporting long hair, once the day of breeching came, at four or five years old, the boundaries between the education of the sexes were firmly laid. To ensure the proper training of conduct and character governesses were employed for girls, while boys were often prepared for entry to public school by private tutors.

Governesses and tutors were in an odd limbo-like position in the household, somewhere mid-stairs: above the servants in social status but definitely below the master and mistress of the house. Governesses usually came from good families and were often spinsters through lack of looks, or, more likely, a dowry. Tutors were frequently clergymen supplementing their meagre stipends. Many governesses and tutors came from the Continent – almost forerunners of the *au pair* – with the undoubted asset of conducting lessons in their native language. They were, as Ursula Wyndham wrote in her autobiography *Astride the Wall*: 'totally isolated. Parents left them in sole command of the schoolroom and treated them with the distant civility they extended to the domestic staff. The governess was intent on proving her gentility, but nobody was interested. The servants were aware of the pretensions of she who presided in the schoolroom, and were in a strong position to put the governess in her place: she was, after all, just another paid employee.'

Even if tutors and governesses had wished to, they were not encouraged to fraternise with the servants and although they may sometimes have been invited to eat with their employers they were discouraged from contributing spontaneously to dining-room conversation. Lady Stanley wrote disparagingly of her children's tutor's lack of social graces: 'We have had the wretched Pedagogue down some evenings but he has such a frightful imbecile manner it is only from humanity we do it.'

When Theresa Parker died at Saltram in November 1775 less than two months after giving birth to a baby girl, also named Theresa, she left a husband, John, the new-born baby and a three-year-old son, Jack. Her sister, Anne Robinson, moved in to help her brother-in-law to bring up the children.

At the age of seven Jack left Saltram and was sent to Hammersmith to attend Dr Kyte's school. In preparation for this move he had been attending the school in Plympton for several months and, rising at 6am, walked the two miles there and back alone. In spite of independence being thrust on him from an early age Jack still showed signs of the little boy, hardly out of childish skirts. Anne wrote of the day he left for Hammersmith: 'He behaved at parting with his usual propriety, though I believe there was a shower [of tears] in the chaise, I took great pains that I should not see it.'

Meanwhile Jack's younger sister, Theresa, remained at Saltram to be instructed in the ways of elegance to prepare her for marriage. For the little girl, Anne Robinson employed a French governess who was obviously a great success:

'Yesterday she [Theresa] gave me one of the short stories translated by herself, into very good English, very exactly done, and very well spelt, and which I have the certainty of knowing must be all her own, as Mad/elle dont understand a word of English. I flatter myself we have got a treasure in her as Governess, she is perfectly good natured, well behave[d], modest and seems sensible, very tall and large, but a good figure, and very decent and creditable looking. Her not speaking English I look upon as her greatest advantage, as she has no temptation to mix with the other servants and be spoiled, she dines with the little girl and is never out of her room but when she walks out with her.'

For Victorian and Edwardian girls, French, German, reading, writing, scripture, embroidery and posture were essential elements of the curriculum of social acceptability. Literature, science and politics were optional extras and depended on parental demand or the whim of the individual governess. A good command of French was judged to be the most important attribute of all and this remained the case from Tudor times to the first half of this century. A young lady with no French was simply *not* a young lady or, as the Countess of Airlie put it to Lady Redesdale, mother of the Mitford girls: 'There is nothing so inferior as a gentlewoman who has no French.' Varying attempts were

Evidently at fault with her lessons, the little girl is being chided by her governess while the boy keeps his eyes on the slate. This painting, done by Helen Allingham in 1885, was included in Happy England, *published in 1903.*
(Mary Evans Picture Library)

made to encourage mini-linguists: the Wyndham children of Petworth in Sussex were made to play games and write riddles and consequences in French while Anthea Mander Lahr, who grew up at Wightwick Manor in Staffordshire in the 1950s, recalls Latin, Greek, French and German vocabulary being pinned to the nursery screen to bring out any latent linguistic tendencies.

Perhaps parents were barking up the wrong tree in preparing their daughters for marriage by training them to be cultured conversationalists. In this respect the last word on feminine appeal *has* to go to Sir George Sitwell expressing his pet theory: 'Nothin' a young man likes so much as a girl who's good at the parallel bars.'

1
Tuesday

2
Wednesday

3
Thursday

4
Friday

5
Saturday

6
Sunday

'If children are reasonably and affectionately educated, scarcely any punishment will be requisite.'

Essays on Practical Education, Maria and Richard Edgeworth, 1789

7
Monday

8
Tuesday

9
Wednesday

10
Thursday

11
Friday

12
Saturday

13
Sunday

'We undertook the tour in order to restore my health and raise our spirits, and to show our children the wonders of the Renaissance, but I confess that more often than not I had to hurry the girls past statues of naked gods that their native innocence might not be impaired; and as for myself, the blushes rose to my cheek when looking on Canova's recumbent figure of Pauline Borghese.'

Mistress of Charlecote: the memoirs of Mary Elizabeth Lucy, edited by Alice Fairfax-Lucy, 1983

FEBRUARY

14
Monday

15
Tuesday

SHROVE TUESDAY

16
Wednesday

ASH WEDNESDAY (LENT BEGINS)

17
Thursday

18
Friday

19
Saturday

20
Sunday

FIRST SUNDAY IN LENT

'We are intellectually still babies; this is perhaps why a baby's facial expression so strangely suggests the professional philosopher.'

George Bernard Shaw (1856–1950)

21
Monday

22
Tuesday

23
Wednesday

24
Thursday

25
Friday

26
Saturday

27
Sunday

28

Monday

In the 1870s when bored with lessons at their home, Osterley Park in Middlesex, the children of the 7th Earl and Countess of Jersey used to amuse themselves by peeling the paint off the Adam-designed chairs in the Etruscan Room.

MARCH

The Good, the Bad and
the Ugly

Lord Curzon of Kedleston (1859–1925) by John Cooke after John Singer Sargent. (National Portrait Gallery)

The Good, the Bad and the Ugly

Soon after Augustus Hare was born in 1834, his widowed aunt wrote to the child's mother asking to be given the small boy. Mrs Hare's reply did not overflow with maternal feeling: 'My dear Maria, how very kind of you! Yes, certainly the baby shall be sent as soon as it is weaned; and, if any one else would like one, would you kindly recollect that we have others.'

This type of detached attitude was by no means unusual in English society, and in fact went back hundreds of years. Since the Middle Ages, the offhand approach of the English to their offspring had been remarked on by bemused visitors to these shores. In 1497, the Venetian envoy to the Court of Henry VII wrote that: 'The want of affection in the English is strongly manifested towards their children; for after having kept them at home till they arrive at the age of seven or nine years at the utmost, they put them out, both males and females, to hard service in the houses of other people, binding them generally for another seven or nine years .... during that time they perform all the most menial offices; and few are born who are exempted from this fate, for everyone, however rich he may be, sends away his children into the houses of others, whilst he, in return, receives those of strangers into his own.'

The envoy was astounded at this custom of 'placing out' which was popular at the time. Basically it meant that parents paid other families to take on their children for a period of apprenticeship learning manners, performing household duties and such like.

Other equally strange practices were to permeate British society then and in later centuries: many children were dispatched to wet nurses at birth (a practice which continued into the eighteenth century and beyond, even Churchill had a wet nurse); others were hastily bundled into the realm of nannies, nursemaids, governesses and tutors – perhaps seeing their parents only once a day – until they magically emerged from the nursery chrysalis as presentable adults ready to take their place in society. It is no surprise that many aristocratic parent-

*The five children of the 2nd Lord Leconfield, photographed with their mother
and a nursemaid at Petworth House in 1883.
(National Trust/Lord Egremont)*

child relationships were odd, producing a host of extraordinary anecdotes. Sir Vauncey Harpur Crewe, 10th Baronet, treated his Calke tenants and employees with more kindness than his own family: it was not unknown for this nineteenth-century Derbyshire magnate to communicate with his children by letters delivered on a silver salver by a footman or by public post. The 6th Duke of Somerset ruled his seventeenth-century household at Petworth in Sussex with an equally bizarre hand, definitely lacking the touch of fatherly love: his children had to stand in his presence at all times, even if he were asleep. The penalties were severe – he had no compunction in axing £20,000 from the inheritance of one daughter who had deigned to take the weight off her feet during his afternoon siesta.

In this complex world of relationships the character of the nurse or nanny could have an enormous impact on her charge and strong bonds often developed between them – for good or bad. Winston Churchill was one child who was devoted to his nanny, Mrs Elizabeth Ann Everest, who became a rock in his and his younger brother's life, while their parents, Lord and Lady Randolph Churchill, busied themselves in high society. Churchill was later to write that Everest had been his 'most dearest and intimate friend' and that he owed her everything. It was Everest who tended him when he was seriously ill with pneumonia, who went to sports days *in loco parentis*, who alerted his mother to excessive caning at prep school and who, in short, was always there for the young boy, giving him unconditional support and affection.

In contrast Lord George Curzon drew a very short straw in the nanny stakes in the sadistic figure of Miss Paraman – the archetypal nanny from hell. After his death in 1925 handwritten notes were found at Curzon's family seat, Kedleston in Derbyshire, telling of his suffering under this woman. They make terrifying reading:

'In her savage moments she was a brutal and vindictive tyrant; and I have often thought since that she must have been insane. She persecuted and beat us in the most cruel way and established over us a system of terrorism so complete that not one of us ever mustered up the courage to walk upstairs and tell our father or mother. She spanked us with the sole of her slipper on the bare back, beat us with her brushes, tied us for long hours to chairs in uncomfortable positions with our hands holding a pole or blackboard behind our backs, shut us up in darkness, practised on us every kind of petty persecution, wounded our pride by dressing us (one in particular) in red shining calico petticoats (I was obliged to make my own) with an immense conical cap on our heads round which, as well as on our breasts and backs, were sewn strips of paper bearing in enormous characters, written by ourselves, the words Liar, Sneak, Coward, Lubber and the like.'

It has been suggested that Curzon was haunted by the spectre of Miss Paraman throughout his life and that much of his obsessiveness in work was a result of the iron hand of his nanny during his formative years. When Miss Paraman died Curzon made a point of attending her funeral perhaps hoping to lay her ghost to rest. However, there can be little doubt that memories of his unhappy childhood stayed with him until his own death.

Life with nanny could be fun or frightening – it was certainly unforgettable.

1
Tuesday

ST DAVID'S DAY

2
Wednesday

3
Thursday

4
Friday

5
Saturday

6
Sunday

'Ours was a strange childhood, though we did not think it strange. Our parents were remote, and therefore admirable. Every day until we went to school was spent under a nanny's eye. Meals, lessons, walks, the nursery routines of bedding and awakening shaped our lives. The high point of each day was our descent to the house at 6 pm, when we would find our mother bent over her current book, patient of our interruption, uncertain how to amuse us.'

Portrait of a Marriage, Nigel Nicolson, 1973

7

Monday

8

Tuesday

9

Wednesday

10

Thursday

11
Friday

12
Saturday

13
Sunday

MOTHERING SUNDAY

'Before carrying me into the drawing-room, this dreadful "Nanny" would pinch and twist
my arm — why, no one knew, unless it was to demonstrate, according to some perverse
reasoning, that her power over me was greater than my parents'. The sobbing and
bawling this treatment invariably evoked understandably puzzled, worried and finally
annoyed them. It would result in my being peremptorily removed from the room before
further embarrassment was inflicted upon them and the other witnesses of this pathetic
scene. Eventually, my mother realised what was wrong, and the nurse was dismissed.'

A King's Story, Duke of Windsor

14
Monday

15
Tuesday

16
Wednesday

17
Thursday

ST PATRICK'S DAY (NORTHERN IRELAND & EIRE)

18
Friday

19
Saturday

20
Sunday

FIFTH SUNDAY IN LENT (PASSION SUNDAY) – SPRING EQUINOX

'One cannot love lumps of flesh, and little infants are nothing more.'

Lord Byron (1788–1824)

21
Monday

22
Tuesday

23
Wednesday

24
Thursday

25
Friday

26
Saturday

27
Sunday

PALM SUNDAY – BRITISH SUMMER TIME BEGINS

After being widowed in 1697 Lady Brownlow ruled her five daughters with a rod of iron. 'Once when the five sisters were enjoying a surreptitious tea-party in one of their rooms, the dreaded footsteps were heard approaching, and to save detection the whole tea equipage was promptly thrown out of the window.'

The Records of the Cust Family, Elizabeth Cust, 1909

28
Monday

29
Tuesday

30
Wednesday

31
Thursday

APRIL

Lost Childhoods

*This portrait by Charles D'Agar of Edward and Catherine, children of
Sir John Harpur of Calke Abbey in Derbyshire, was painted in 1718 when
Edward was only five years old.
(NTPL/Christopher Hurst)*

Lost Childhoods

hildhood as we know it passed as quickly as an April shower for many in earlier centuries. Until the eighteenth-century 'Age of the Enlightenment', infants were regarded as inferior adults brimming over with original sin who needed to be purged of their defects as rapidly as possible and put on the road to adulthood to save them from eternal damnation. Babies were encased at birth in swaddling bands to straighten their wayward limbs. Crawling was regarded as animal-like and unnatural, so tiny infants careered around in baby-walkers made of hoops of willow. Even affection was often denied – for their own good of course – as kissing and cuddling were thought to breed and spread disease. Few concessions were made for children: they shared the same clothes and books as adults and were encouraged to assume adult roles as soon as possible. Rocking horses were considered acceptable 'toys' because they prepared children to ride, while high chairs meant that children could be pushed up to eat at the same table as adults. For poorer families, adult responsibilities came quickly: as soon as children could walk they were put out to work, and girls often took on the role of mother to their younger siblings if their own mother died or was absent at full-time work. Their own marriage and experiences of childbirth were only a matter of time.

Perhaps of all these practices the most alien to us today is the concept of child marriage, prevalent during the Middle Ages and beyond throughout all ranks of society. There are countless records of babes in arms being brought to church to be married off to equally young spouses with either parent or priest reciting the vows if the child was too young to talk. One fifteenth-century account tells of an uncooperative three-year-old groom: 'Before he had got through his lesson [the wedding vows], the child declared he would learn no more that day. The priest answered: "You must speak a little more, and then go play you."'

It was perhaps more understandable for the landed classes to wish to preserve and amalgamate their wealth through advantageous marriages. Heirs and children were but pawns in the marriage game of property and influence. When Joscelyn Percy, the 11th Earl of Northumberland and owner of Petworth in Sussex and other estates, died in 1670 his heir was a three-year-old girl, Elizabeth. As a result she became instrumental in her grandmother's ambitious plan to make the best marriage possible to consolidate the Percy fortunes. At the age of twelve Elizabeth walked down the aisle with Henry Cavendish, the son and heir of the Duke of Newcastle, only to become a widow a year later in 1680. Not given much chance to wear widow's weeds she was married off the following year to the immensely wealthy Thomas Thynne of Longleat in Wiltshire. Having entered her teens and already on her second marriage Elizabeth obviously considered herself a woman of the world and took a Swedish lover, rejoicing in the suitably romantic name of Count Charles von Königsmark. Elizabeth's girlish charms must have bewitched the Count as he was hot-blooded enough to arrange the murder of Thynne who was brutally attacked by gunmen while travelling in his coach along Pall Mall less than three months after his marriage to Elizabeth. Thynne's tomb in Westminster Abbey commemorates the gruesome deed with a bas-relief of the ambush. In May 1682, a mere three months after Thynne's demise, Elizabeth was married to her third and final husband, Charles Seymour, the 6th Duke of Somerset, who fathered a male heir the following year, enjoyed Elizabeth's inheritance, remodelled Petworth and outlived his wife by 26 years.

Arabella Stuart, the granddaughter of Elizabeth Shrewsbury (better known as Bess of Hardwick), suffered the opposite fate to Elizabeth Percy and was forced to remain a spinster for most of her life precisely *because* of her lineage. Through her father, Charles Lennox, Arabella had a claim to the throne after Elizabeth I's death. There were talks of the Queen naming her as heir, secret marriage matches, plots to overthrow the Crown, kidnap conspiracies and such like. Small wonder that the child grew up with an inflated opinion of herself as the focus of national speculation. As a teenager she went to court but proved unpopular and arrogant and was sent back in disgrace to the wilds of Derbyshire and her grandmother. Elizabeth, who had to approve any marriage which involved a claimant to the throne, vetoed all possible suitors, fearful of a takeover, while Bess of Hardwick, anxious to keep on the right side of the Queen, kept her granddaughter practically under armed guard. One of her letters informs Lord Burghley of security arrangements at Hardwick:

'Arbelle walks not late; at such time as she shall take the air it shall

Because of her claims to the English throne, the childhood of Lady Arabella Stuart was fleeting. This anonymous portrait showing her aged 23 months, hangs in Hardwick Hall, Derbyshire. (NTPL/R. A. Wilsher)

be near the house and well attended on. She goeth not to anybody's house at all. I see her almost every hour of the day. She lieth in my bedchamber.'

Hardly surprisingly not much love was lost between Arabella and her grandmother and the young woman became desperate to escape. She engineered a secret marriage to Edward Seymour which would strengthen her claim to the throne. The plot was uncovered, and Arabella, questioned by the Queen's officers, lied over and over again, so incurring Elizabeth's wrath while Bess fumed over her grand-daughter's recklessness and the souring of relations between her and the monarch. The troublesome girl was taken into custody but after the deaths of Elizabeth and Bess she married Seymour secretly and tried to flee the country. She was captured and spent her final years in the Tower of London dying in 1615 a bitter, lonely and, by all accounts, slightly mad 40-year-old. A life which had promised much had been ruined through the bad luck of her parentage.

1
Friday

GOOD FRIDAY (BANK HOLIDAY UK EXCLUDING SCOTLAND)

2
Saturday

3
Sunday

EASTER DAY

'I think she hath some strange vapours to her brain.'

Sir Robert Cecil (*c*.1563–1612) of Arabella Stuart

4
Monday

EASTER MONDAY (BANK HOLIDAY UK EXCLUDING SCOTLAND)

5
Tuesday

6
Wednesday

7
Thursday

8
Friday

9
Saturday

10
Sunday

Lord George Hay wrote in 1707 about his infant nephew's prowess in moving: he 'runs up and down the room in a machine made of willows but my lady the Countess takes care that he does not stress himself with walking too much.'

11
Monday

12
Tuesday

13
Wednesday

14
Thursday

15
Friday

16
Saturday

17
Sunday

'Adam and Eve had many advantages, but the principal one was that
they escaped teething.'

Pudd'nhead Wilson, Mark Twain (1835–1910)

18
Monday

19
Tuesday

20
Wednesday

21
Thursday

22
Friday

23
Saturday

ST GEORGE'S DAY

24
Sunday

25
Monday

26
Tuesday

27
Wednesday

28
Thursday

29
Friday

30
Saturday

'I love children – especially when they cry, for then someone takes them away.'
Nancy Mitford (1904–73)

NOTES

MAY

Swaddling Bands to
Sailor Suits

Swaddling Bands to Sailor Suits

rom Roman times babies started off life uncomfortably bound in swaddling bands in the misplaced belief that as a result they would grow up strong and straight-limbed. By the eighteenth century people were beginning to question the practice. Theresa Parker of Saltram in Devon, whose children Jack and Theresa were born in 1772 and 1775, complained that 'a child is no sooner born that it is bound up as firmly as an Egyptian mummy in folds of linen.' Jean-Jacques Rousseau, in his novel *Emile* (1762), had a character say, 'Away with swaddling clothes, give the child large and flowing robes that leave all his limbs free.'

In the Middle Ages once a child had escaped the restrictions of swaddling bands, it was dressed to distinguish its sex. From the sixteenth century, however, all children were 'shortened' – or dressed in flannel petticoats and frocks with boys and girls being indistinguishable until the day of breeching. This sign of a boy's move into adulthood (at the age of four or five) was customarily marked by great celebrations while the child was encased in a miniature set of man's clothing with little concession for play and ease of movement. Portraits show just how restrictive such clothes must have been. A painting (1718) of the two eldest children of Sir John Harpur, 4th Baronet, hanging at the family home of Calke Abbey in Derbyshire (p.54), shows expressions of seriousness beyond their ten and eight years as they pose in their finery. Girls tended to be dressed in exact copies of women's clothes which, in Tudor times, were often bedecked in jewels and extremely ornate – a picture of Arabella Stuart (p.57), the granddaughter of Bess of Hardwick, at Hardwick Hall in Derbyshire, portrays Arabella at the age of two wearing jewellery of gold chains

OPPOSITE *The mother in this Victorian family group, painted by James Sant, is Caroline, wife of the 3rd Earl of Edgcumbe, who settled at Cotehele in Cornwall after the death of her husband in 1861. The elder child is wearing fashionable plaid. (Plymouth City Museum and Art Gallery, Mount Edgcumbe House Collection)*

Sailor suits were popular after Queen Victoria commissioned one for her eldest son, Bertie. (Mary Evans Picture Library)

over a dress with elaborately embroidered sleeves and bodice. A portrait of four of the thirteen children of Thomas Lucy III (d.1640) of Charlecote in Warwickshire shows the sitters wearing clothes of rich brocaded material. The eldest three have delicate lace cuffs, collars and ruffs and their fashionably frizzed hair is dotted with lacey ornaments, while the baby sits in a chair wearing a plainer bonnet and cuffs. The two younger children wear protective white pinafores over their dresses, clearly even children dressed as adults still threw their food around. On the shoulders of the three eldest children's clothes are leading strings made from the same fabric unobtrusively sewn into the design, showing that even such unnaturally grown-up looking girls were still children and occasionally needed guiding and restraining.

Victorian childhood fashion took the form of a fancy dress parade: including miniature soldiers, cavaliers, Scots and sailors. The last two were the most enduring. The Victorian mania for highland dress, tartans, Tam o'Shanters and all things checked and plaid was prompted by the popularity of Walter Scott's novels, endorsed by Victoria's and Albert's love affair with Scotland. Unless they were true Scots, no self-respecting adults were going to swathe themselves in tartan with all the trimmings, so this treat was reserved for children and nursery wardrobes rapidly filled with sporrans, kilts and Glengarry caps. Not all were convinced. In *The Science of Dress*, published in 1885, Ada Ballin warned parents of the dangers of kilt-wearing for boys, quoting the example of a six-year-old who had not grown since the age of three as a result of revealing his knees to the world. In spite of this dire warning tartanmania continued.

When children were not being dressed as mini-Caledonians they were appearing as jolly Jack Tars – again thanks to the fashion set by the royal family. In 1846 Victoria had commissioned the ship's tailor of the royal yacht to make a sailor suit for her eldest son, Bertie, and he was painted by Winterhalter wearing his simplified naval regalia. The uniform had the advantage of being adaptable for girls who wore pleated skirts instead of trousers. The same harsh critic of the kilt's restricting powers had no such qualms about the sailor's suit describing it as 'a very pretty and nice dress for boys . . . which by its looseness allows free movement, and is very durable and covers all the limbs.'

Even more comfortable and roomy were the clothes recommended by the Aesthetic and Arts and Crafts movements which resurrected smocked dresses in the 1870s and 1880s, so giving children ample space for movement. Bright colours were considered 'unartistic', so clothes tended to be in muted tones described witheringly by one commentator as 'cobwebby grey velvet with a tender bloom like cold gravy'. Old gold was a popular colour. Edy, the young daughter of the renowned Victorian actress, Ellen Terry, was given a doll 'dressed in a violent pink silk'. To her mother's relief her daughter had obviously inherited aesthetic principles and Edy refused to play with her new toy, describing it as 'vulgar'.

The world of children's fashion had come of age.

NOTES

1

Sunday

The cult of baby worship could be an expensive business. In 1821 it was reported that 'Paris, Brussels, London and Vienna had been ransacked' at a cost of nearly £2,000 for the layette of the future 5th Marquess of Londonderry.

2
Monday

MAY DAY (BANK HOLIDAY UK)

3
Tuesday

4
Wednesday

5
Thursday

6
Friday

7
Saturday

8
Sunday

9
Monday

10
Tuesday

11
Wednesday

12
Thursday

ASCENSION DAY

13
Friday

14
Saturday

15
Sunday

SUNDAY AFTER ASCENSION

A bit of a talcum?
Is always walcum

Reflection on babies, Ogden Nash (1902–71)

16
Monday

17
Tuesday

18
Wednesday

19
Thursday

20
Friday

21
Saturday

22
Sunday

WHIT SUNDAY (PENTECOST)

'Sunday, November 1, 1801. Hartley breeched dancing to the jingling of the money – but eager & solemn Joy, not his usual whirl-about-gladness.'

From the notebooks of Samuel Taylor Coleridge, describing the breeching of his eldest child, Hartley, born in 1796.

23
Monday

24
Tuesday

25
Wednesday

26
Thursday

27
Friday

28
Saturday

29
Sunday

TRINITY SUNDAY

30
Monday

31
Tuesday

'My mother groan'd, my father wept,
Into the dangerous world I leapt;
Helpless, naked, piping loud;
Like a fiend hid in a cloud.

Struggling in my father's hands,
Striving against my swaddling bands,
Round and weary I thought best
To sulk upon my mother's breast.'

Infant Sorrow, William Blake (1757–1827)

JUNE

The Clergyman and
the Sweep

SWEEP, SWEEP!

*Two small boys employed as chimney sweeps tout for trade as their employer
cries 'Sweep, Sweep!'. From* Cries of London *by J. Harris, 1804.
(Mary Evans Picture Library)*

The Clergyman and the Sweep

The heath was full of bilberries and whinberries; but they were only in flower yet, for it was June. And as for water, who can find that on the top of a limestone rock? Now and then he passed by a deep dark swallow-hole, going down into the earth, as if it was the chimney of some dwarf's house underground; and more than once, as he passed, he could hear water falling, trickling, tinkling, many many feet below. How he longed to get down to it, and cool his poor baked lips! But brave little chimney-sweep as he was, he dared not climb down such chimneys as those.

 t is said that the Reverend Charles Kingsley's inspiration for the setting of the opening chapters of his classic children's tale *The Water Babies*, published in 1863, came from the ghostly, limestone pavement landscape of the Yorkshire Dales and, in particular, Malham Tarn near Settle. Kingsley had stayed near Skipton in the months before writing his story and 'Vendale' and 'Harthover' are drawn from his impressions of this unusual landscape. However it is not for its setting that *The Water Babies* is remembered. The tale was written by Kingsley in a crusading spirit on two counts: to highlight the desperate plight of child sweeps and to promote imaginative and fantasy books for children as an alternative to the fad for dull self-improving tomes.

Kingsley felt passionately about the constructive powers of imagination and recreation in children's lives and was concerned that their minds were in danger of being stifled by rigid Victorian educational principles. Tom's discovery of the Isle of Tomtoddies, where a notice declares 'Playthings not allowed here', reveals a nightmare land where children have metamorphosed into turnips and spend their lives, spurred on by parents, learning useless facts until their brains burst. Tom is told the sorry state of affairs by the stick of Roger Ascham:

'You see,' said the stick, 'they were as pretty little children once as you could wish to see, and might have been so still if they had only been left to grow up like human beings, and then handed over to me; but their foolish fathers and mothers, instead of letting them pick flowers, and make dirtpies, and get birds' nests, and dance round the gooseberry bush, as little children should, kept them always at lessons, working, working, working, learning weekday lessons all weekdays, and Sunday lessons all Sunday, and weekly examinations every Saturday, and monthly examinations every month, and yearly examinations every year, everything seven times over, as if once was not enough, and enough as good as a feast – till their brains grew big, and their bodies grew small, and they were all changed into turnips, with little but water inside; and still their foolish parents actually pick the leaves off them as fast as they grow, lest they should have anything green about them.'

For all Kingsley's moralising and sermonising throughout *The Water Babies* the most enduring images of the tale are, of course, the figure of Tom, who 'cried when he had to climb the dark flues, rubbing his poor knees and elbows raw; and when the soot got into his eyes, which it did every day in the week', and his evil master, Grimes. Much of the detail for this part of the story was gained from Kingsley's personal contact with James Seaward, the boy who used to sweep his own chimneys at Eversley Rectory in Devon and who, after he had risen in life to become Mayor of Wokingham, claimed to be the original Tom, saying he knew what it was like to 'come down the dark flue not only covered with soot, but with blood also, from the rough climbing with knees and hands and elbows'. Seaward was lucky to survive to adulthood – many boy sweeps contracted a variety of diseases from their work: skin cancer and eye problems caused by the soot; breathing complications connected with inhaling a daily dose of charcoal, sulphur and ammonia, while others sought refuge in alcohol. Kingsley was a keen Christian Socialist and so deeply concerned with these social issues – although apparently not enough to stop his own chimney being swept by James Seaward.

In 1863 the government produced a report on child labour spurred on by the selfless work of Lord Shaftesbury who had vividly described the stunted bodies of child chimney sweeps and miners as 'a mass of crooked alphabets'. It was amid this atmosphere of social concern that Kingsley wrote Tom's story.

The book seems to have helped both the cause of the sweeps *and* Kingsley's plea for more inventive children's literature. The year after *The Water Babies* was published Parliament passed an act forbidding the employment of young children as sweeps. In 1865, Lewis Carroll's *Alice's Adventures in Wonderland* was published – a book of sheer imagination if ever there was one. The Water Baby had done his work.

An illustration by Jessie Willcox Smith from a 1920 edition of
The Water Babies *by Charles Kingsley, showing Tom caught in a fishing net.*
(Mary Evans Picture Library)

JUNE

1
Wednesday

2
Thursday

3
Friday

4
Saturday

5
Sunday

'When my mother died I was very young
And my father sold me while yet my tongue
Could scarcely cry weep, weep, weep, weep
And so your chimneys I sweep and in soot I sleep.'

The Chimney Sweeper, Songs of Innocence, William Blake (1757–1827)

6
Monday

BANK HOLIDAY (EIRE)

7
Tuesday

8
Wednesday

9
Thursday

10
Friday

11
Saturday

QUEEN'S OFFICIAL BIRTHDAY

12
Sunday

'The evils of the employ are doubled by intemperance. The sweeps who travel through the country are especially drunken; and the lads acquire a craving for liquor from their habit of receiving beer at every house they serve. Many chimney-sweeps die in youth. Surely this shocking and unnatural occupation ought to be abolished!'

The Effects of the Principal Arts, Trades and Professions on Health, C. Turner Thrackrah

13
Monday

14
Tuesday

15
Wednesday

16
Thursday

17
Friday

18
Saturday

19
Sunday

FATHER'S DAY

'The dangerous practice of forcing little chimney sweeps to climb up a niche on the outside of St George's Church, Hanover Square, still continues. A dirty brute, was yesterday employed for near two hours in forcing a child, at the risk of his life, to climb up the place alluded to; sometimes by sending another lad to poke him up, by putting his head underneath him, and at other times by pricking him with a pin fastened to the end of a stick. The poor child, in the struggles to keep himself from falling, had rubbed the skin from his knees and elbows, while the perspiration arising from fear and exertion covered his face and breast as if water had been thrown upon him.'

The Lady Magazine, 31 December, 1802

20
Monday

21
Tuesday

MIDSUMMER'S DAY – THE LONGEST DAY

22
Wednesday

23
Thursday

24
Friday

25
Saturday

26
Sunday

'A child's spirit is like a child, you can never catch it by running after it; you must stand still, and for love, it will soon come back.'

The Crucible, Arthur Miller (b.1915)

27
Monday

28
Tuesday

29
Wednesday

30
Thursday

JULY

The Realm of Anywhere

Seated girl in a blue dress *by J. Frayer,*
hanging at Standen, West Sussex.
(NTPL/Derrick E. Whitty)

The Realm of Anywhere

current parental concern is judging the effect of horror films, video-nasties and monstrous toys on children's lives and their developing imaginations. However, a brief glance at the books which may have graced a Victorian nursery bookshelf shows that a dose of horror is by no means a newcomer to children's 'entertainment'. Gustav Doré who illustrated Perrault's fairy tales had a particular feel for the nightmarish image: his Puss-in-Boots is no cuddly moggy but a wild-eyed, sharp-fanged, rabid buccaneer type, with a collection of dead mice dangling from his belt and a necklace of sparrows' heads. Then there was, of course, the infamous *Struwwelpeter* which was translated into English from the German in 1848 with the beguiling sub-title of 'Pretty Stories and Funny Pictures for Little Children'. It became one of the best-selling nursery titles of all time. Between its covers children could read goggle-eyed of the horrid fates which awaited them if they misbehaved.

The National Trust can lay no claim to connections with either of the above horror tales but does have its fair share of children's literary links. Most famous must be Beatrix Potter, who donated many farms in the Lake District, bought with the proceeds of her highly successful books. But then there is also Angela Brazil, the creator of many 'jolly hockey sticks' schoolgirl tales, who left land in Cornwall to the Trust on her death in 1947. Beatrix Potter was not alone in gaining inspiration from land now owned by the Trust: Arthur Ransome lived near Pin Mill on the Suffolk coast while writing *We Didn't Mean to Go To Sea* amongst other titles in his East Anglian children's adventure series; Charles Kingsley was inspired to write *The Water Babies* after visiting Malham Tarn in North Yorkshire, while in contemporary literature, Helen Cresswell based her novel *Moondial* on the ghostly goings-on at Belton House in Lincolnshire.

Outside the realm of reading, imagination has always had a large part in playtime, often resulting in children inventing unusual variants on well-known games. In *Astride the Wall*, Ursula Wyndham

A corner of Seventh Heaven, the name Charles Wade gave to his favourite room at Snowshill Manor, Gloucestershire, where many childhood toys are kept. (NTPL/Andreas von Einsiedel)

recalls playing a game of one-upmanship with her brother and friends at Petworth which involved thumbing through the pages of *Country Life* and awarding marks 'for either knowing or being related to the social celebrities whose photographs appeared on the opening page.'

Most of our knowledge of children's play in the past comes from toys and games that have survived. Snowshill Manor in Gloucestershire, the home of the compulsive collector, Charles Wade, is a chest of eclectic treasures and includes a room in the attic dedicated to childhood. He named it Seventh Heaven after his belief that this state could only 'be attained in childhood before schools and schoolmasters have been able to destroy the greatest of treasures, imagination'. Many of the objects are toys which he played with as a boy in the last decade of the nineteenth century, including a model yacht, train, South African covered wagon and a Noah's Ark. The nursery at Erddig in

North Wales still displays the toys played with by the Yorke children over the generations, including the wooden train built for Simon Yorke's fifth birthday in 1908 by the estate carpenter, William Gittins. Gittins is remembered in verse – the hallmark of the Yorke family. From the eulogy penned by Philip Yorke II it appears that the flexible carpenter would mend as well as build toys:

> For all repairs both great and small
> On Mr. Gittins straight we call
> Nor does his talent e'er despise
> The toys that charm our Children's eyes.

Calke Abbey in Derbyshire was to prove an unlikely source of childhood memorabilia. When Calke was taken over by the National Trust in 1985 it was described as a time-capsule, a house where time had stood still since the nineteenth century. Every room revealed extraordinary treasures: no child had lived at Calke since the 1920s yet the Schoolroom was still furnished with a doll's house and rocking horse. Better still the chests-of-drawers in the same room were found to contain dozens of carefully wrapped dolls dating from Victorian times, sets of lead soldiers still in their boxes and many examples of children's books and games which had lain undisturbed for years.

Outdoor entertainments for children have also left their mark. Children were taught to ride at an early age, and having mastered the nursery rocking horse would move on to the real thing. Caroline Wiggett recalls her early nineteenth-century childhood days at The Vyne in Hampshire and the thrill of riding in the local hunt:

'A very great excitement to the household was the days the hounds met . . . everybody turned out of the house and when a child, dear me! what a wild creature I was, nothing daunted me at hearing the bugle, out I was over hedge and ditch tally-hoing at the top of my voice. Uncle C said that when Cal was running no need of horses and hounds *She* would kill the fox.'

Others pursued less energetic outdoor pastimes. In the mid nineteenth century, Mary Elizabeth Lucy, of Charlecote in Warwickshire, built a miniature thatched summerhouse for her children and furnished it with child-sized tables; it proved to have enduring appeal and was used by her children's children who referred to it as Granny's summerhouse. One hundred years later Churchill was to do the same for his youngest child, Mary, by building the Marycot in the grounds of Chartwell, their Kent family home. It was, needless to say, constructed of brick.

1
Friday

2
Saturday

3
Sunday

'Here was a Kingdom beyond the ken of Grown-Ups, all free from that overlooking eye. This happy realm under the table and round the skirtings. How intimate one was with the legs of furniture, textures and patterns of carpets.'

Days Far Away, Charles Wade (1883–1956)

4
Monday

5
Tuesday

6
Wednesday

7
Thursday

8
Friday

9
Saturday

10
Sunday

'Treasure beyond measure,
Imaginative mind,
Magic key to open,
The Realm of Anywhere.'

Days Far Away, Charles Wade (1883–1956)

11
Monday

12
Tuesday

BANK HOLIDAY (NORTHERN IRELAND)

13
Wednesday

14
Thursday

15
Friday

16
Saturday

17
Sunday

In 1938, a catalogue from the London toy shop, Hamley's, described current models of dolls' houses in the style of estate agents' particulars for actual properties:

'Picturesque country house with six rooms and hall. Fitted with seven electric lights. All windows and doors open. Fireplaces in all rooms.'

18
Monday

19
Tuesday

20
Wednesday

21
Thursday

22
Friday

23
Saturday

24
Sunday

25
Monday

26
Tuesday

27
Wednesday

28
Thursday

29
Friday

30
Saturday

31
Sunday

'May I join you in the doghouse, Rover?
I wish to retire till the party's over.'

Children's Party, Ogden Nash (1902–71)

AUGUST

Tea and Torture

Tea and Torture

or the first years of her life, Vita Sackville-West – later to gain fame for her writing, gardening and unconventional marriage – lived at Knole, the magnificent medieval house set in acres of ancient deer park outside Sevenoaks in Kent. Vita, an only child, was able to roam the grounds and dark winding corridors of the house letting both herself and her imagination run wild.

Vita's mother, Victoria, was the illegitimate daughter of the 2nd Lord Sackville. Then, in 1890, she married her first cousin, Lionel Sackville-West, the heir to the Sackville title and the estate. In spite of Sackville ancestry on both sides, Vita knew that she could never inherit the estate because of her sex and that, on her father's death, Knole would go to her uncle and his family. Perhaps this example of sex discrimination concerning matters of inheritance encouraged Vita to be as boyish as possible in her youth.

When Vita was a small child Victoria was able to mould her to be the attractive daughter she had desired. She could dress her up in pretty, frilly clothes, curl her obstinately straight hair, give her dolls to play with and parade her in front of visiting dignitaries confident that her little daughter would provoke admiring remarks. Vita was later to write that her mother 'loved me when I was baby, but I don't think she loved me as a child, nor do I blame her'.

By the age of seven the strength of Vita's personality was becoming clear and the tomboy emerged with a vengeance. Victoria's attempt to start a dancing class at Knole for her daughter's contemporaries resulted in Vita bullying the other children. Soon any child with any sense would refuse an invitation to tea at Knole knowing that the fare would include torture as well as tea-cakes. The four Battiscombe sisters from Sevenoaks were particular victims: their brother allied

OPPOSITE *The Grand Staircase with the Sackville leopards at Knole where Vita Sackville-West roamed wild as a child. (NTPL/Horst Kolo)*

Vita Sackville-West and her mother Lady Sackville at Knole, Kent, in 1900.
(Nigel Nicolson)

with Vita – who now favoured khaki rather than frills – as the helpless girls were tied to trees, thrashed with nettles, had their noses stuffed with putty and their mouths gagged with handkerchiefs. Adults and animals were not safe either: Vita would hide in trees and drop birds' eggs on the heads of people below and enforce population control on her pet rabbits by throwing superfluous baby bunnies over the garden wall. It is no surprise that her father, Lionel Sackville-West, was frequently heard to remark: 'I wish that Vita was more *normal*'.

By the age of ten Vita had metamorphosed from a delightful toddler into 'an unsociable and unnatural girl with long black hair and long black legs and very short frocks and very dirty nails and torn clothes' (her own description). During one holiday in Scotland Vita was made to keep a diary in French as a punishment for wrestling with a hall-boy, but as a rule she was allowed to run wild: 'I practically lived at the farm, where I built myself a shanty. I was happy there. Mother was sensible about me. I was always out, either with the guns, or with the farmer's boys, or by myself.' The situation seemed irretrievable and Victoria accepted that her dream of raising an elegant society beauty was over, although ironically Vita did turn into a strikingly beautiful young woman. According to Vita's recollections her mother often cut her to the quick by saying 'she couldn't bear to look at me because I was so ugly'. Apart from possessing a sharp tongue Victoria appears to have been of somewhat fiery character – no doubt inheriting the Latin temperament of her Spanish mother who had stolen the 2nd Lord Sackville's heart. A stream of nannies and governesses passed in and out of Knole, each dismissed for varying reasons. Vita's favourite and trusted nanny was accused by Victoria of the unlikely crime of consuming three dozen quails which were missing from the kitchens. She was sacked on the spot.

In 1913, on the eve of her wedding to Harold Nicolson in the Chapel at Knole, Vita wrote a poem recalling her solitary, but fascinating, childhood:

> 'Pictures and galleries and empty rooms,
> Small wonder that my games were played alone,
> Half of the rambling house to call my own,
> And wooded gardens with mysterious glooms ...
> This I remember, and the carven oak
> The long and polished floors, the many stairs,
> The heraldic windows, and the velvet chairs
> And portraits that I knew so well, they almost spoke.'

She conveniently omitted any mention of the torture behind the rhododendrons.

1
Monday

BANK HOLIDAY (SCOTLAND & EIRE)

2
Tuesday

3
Wednesday

4
Thursday

5
Friday

6
Saturday

7
Sunday

Lady Sackville to her daughter, Vita:

'One must always tell the truth, darling, if one can, but not *all* the truth; *toute vérité n'est pas bonne à dire.*'

Children of Great Country Houses, Adeline Hartcup, 1982

8
Monday

9
Tuesday

10
Wednesday

11
Thursday

12
Friday

13
Saturday

14
Sunday

'I kept my nerves under control, and made a great deal of being hearty, and as like a boy as possible.'

Vita Sackville-West from *Portrait of a Marriage*, Nigel Nicolson, 1973

15
Monday

16
Tuesday

17
Wednesday

18
Thursday

19
Friday

20
Saturday

21
Sunday

22
Monday

23
Tuesday

24
Wednesday

25
Thursday

26
Friday

27
Saturday

28
Sunday

'... there on the shelves at home ... the books awaited .... Each was a crystal in which the child dreamed he saw life moving.'

The Lost Childhood and other essays, Grahame Greene (1904–91)

29
Monday

BANK HOLIDAY (ENGLAND, WALES & NORTHERN IRELAND)

30
Tuesday

31
Wednesday

'Parentage is a very important profession, but no test of fitness for it is ever imposed in the interest of the children.'

Everybody's Political What's What, George Bernard Shaw (1856–1950)

SEPTEMBER

Paupers and Paternalism

Paupers and Paternalism

uarry Bank Mill at Styal nestles in an idyllic Cheshire river valley, as it has done for the past two hundred years. The beautiful setting belies the fact that this was one of the most productive cotton mills to spring from the Industrial Revolution. It was a natural choice for young Samuel Greg, a Mancunian entrepreneur, who recognised the potential of the site for a water-powered textile mill when he surveyed the countryside surrounding Manchester in 1783.

The only major problem for mills in a rural setting was that of labour. The increasing enclosure of land and the resulting loss of livelihood forced large numbers of rural families into the cities in search of work or on to the mercy of parish authorities whose resources were soon overstretched. It was not long before mill owners and parish overseers realised that a simple 'back-scratching' solution was the answer to both their problems. Wherever possible the parish authorities were anxious to relieve themselves of any financial burden, such as providing for pauper children, while the mill owners were eager to find a cheap source of labour. Parish authorities who were approached by mills lying outside their boundaries were even more ready to cooperate for, if the worker lost his job, he would be the responsibility of the mill's parish rather than the parish from which he had come.

Samuel Greg and his descendants tapped this source of labour and from 1790 to 1840 pauper apprentices formed approximately one-third of the workforce of the family cotton empire at Quarry Bank Mill. Greg was strict in his demands before signing an apprentice's indenture: a premium was paid to him per child for the transfer of responsibility; he preferred girl workers as he found them 'less truculent than the boys' and he insisted that each new apprentice arrived at the Mill with a specified set of clothing. In return the Mill's part of the bargain was to

OPPOSITE *The Apprentice House at Quarry Bank Mill, Styal, in Cheshire, was built in 1790. At its peak, it housed 90 children. (NTPL/Mike Williams)*

'allow unto the said Apprentice ... sufficient Meat, Drink, Apparel, Lodging, Washing, and other Things necessary and fit for an Apprentice'. The children were housed at the Apprentice House, built in 1790 and extended over the years to house at its peak 90 children.

Samuel Greg's theory that girls were less truculent than boys seems to have foundered in the case of Esther Price, an apprentice at Styal in the 1830s. In August 1836 she had been brought before the magistrates for beating up another apprentice and then compounded her sins soon after by running away from the Mill one Saturday night. She took with her as her accomplice Lucy Garner, another apprentice. Lucy, obviously not as streetwise as Esther, was caught the following Thursday and brought back to the Apprentice House where, as punishment, she was locked in a bare attic with a diet of porridge for three days. After ten days on the run Esther returned and took Lucy's place in the lockup, but as she had been away longer her punishment was more severe: a week of solitary confinement and this time the room's windows were boarded up. Matters worsened for Esther when Mrs Timperley, the house superintendent, died of apoplexy. The thought of being locked up in the same house as the corpse scared Esther witless and she pleaded, successfully, to be released to complete her sentence another time. In fact she was let off the rest of her punishment.

Beating does not appear to have played a part in Styal disciplining, perhaps because Greg realised that a beaten child would not be capable of working efficiently. The most effective deterrent – for girls at least – seems to have been hair-cropping which publicly humiliated them without reducing their ability to work. The apprentices appear to have been given a relatively healthy and varied diet: meat was served three times a week and milk apparently formed a substantial part of the diet. The Apprentice House also had an extensive vegetable garden which provided the children with nutritious fresh fruit and vegetables.

In spite of these benefits, life could hardly have been described as a bed of roses. Apprentices had to work from six in the morning to seven in the evening daily except Sundays; even Sundays were strictly controlled and involved a two-mile walk to church followed by school in the afternoon. During the week the work was monotonous and more often than not could be dangerous. Because of their size, children were frequently used to crawl between machines to free tangles and jams, and accidents were common. One apprentice, Thomas Priestly, tells how he lost a finger in the machinery: 'there was a great deal of cotton in the machine, one of the wheels caught my finger and tore it off, it was the forefinger of my left hand. I was attended by the surgeon of the factory Mr Holland and in about six weeks I recovered.' Other apprentices were not so lucky and fatal accidents were not unknown.

The Health and Morals of Apprentices Act, passed in 1802, ordered that apprentices should spend some time each day 'in the usual hours of work learning Reading, Writing and Arithmetic'. This was translated loosely at Quarry Bank Mill, and one runaway's statement in 1806 shows that education definitely took a second place to any mill work. In reply to questioning by magistrates on his capture, Joseph Sefton detailed the educational provisions:

'We had school every night but we used to attend about once a week (besides Sundays when we all attended) eight at a time. I wanted to go oftener to school than twice a week including Sundays but Richard Bamford would not let me go tho' the mill had stopped but this was the time that the straps and frames wanted mending.'

Ironically, one of Quarry Bank Mill's finest assets today is its educational facilities. Under the guidance of the Quarry Bank Mill Trust, an independent charity which leases the Mill from the National Trust, the Mill and Apprentice House have come to life once again to become a living exhibit in the history of the Industrial Revolution. Through an imaginative scheme, school children are given an opportunity to experience life as a mill apprentice for a day – though they do not, of course, have to endanger their fingers by crawling under heavy mill machinery.

A modern-day child experiences the life of a nineteenth-century apprentice at Styal. (NT/Mike Williams)

1
Thursday

2
Friday

3
Saturday

4
Sunday

'We came to Taunton ... there was not a Child in the Town, or in the Villages round it, of above five Years old, but, if it was not neglected by its parents, and untaught, could earn its own Bread.'

A Tour thro' the Island of Great Britain Vol.II, Daniel Defoe, 1724

5
Monday

6
Tuesday

7
Wednesday

8
Thursday

9
Friday

10
Saturday

11
Sunday

12
Monday

13
Tuesday

14
Wednesday

15
Thursday

16
Friday

17
Saturday

18
Sunday

'There is always one moment in childhood when the door opens and lets the future in.'

The Power and the Glory, Grahame Greene (1904–91)

19
Monday

20
Tuesday

21
Wednesday

22
Thursday

23
Friday

AUTUMN EQUINOX

24
Saturday

25
Sunday

'One of the most obvious facts about grown-ups, to a child, is that they have forgotten what it is like to be a child.'

The Man Who Loved Children, Randall Jarrell (1914–65)

26
Monday

27
Tuesday

28
Wednesday

29
Thursday

MICHAELMAS DAY

30
Friday

'The events of childhood do not pass but repeat themselves like seasons of the year.'

Eleanor Farjeon (1881–1965)

NOTES

OCTOBER

The House of Desolation

WE ARE ALL

BORN PRINCES.

LE ROI S'AMUSE

AYAH & BEARER

N. INDIA.

A watercolour drawing by Rudyard Kipling's father, Lockwood,
illustrates how doting native servants indulged their charges.
Lockwood Kipling was appointed Professor of Architectural
Sculpture at Bombay School of Art in 1865.
(University of Sussex/National Trust)

The House of Desolation

———

udyard Kipling bought Bateman's in East Sussex in 1902. It is a quintessentially English Jacobean house, deep in the countryside, and in its porch Kipling hung a wrought-iron bell pull 'in the hope that other children might also feel happy when they rang it'. The bell had originally hung at the London home of Kipling's uncle, the famous pre-Raphaelite artist Sir Edward Burne-Jones, and for Kipling the bell pull symbolised an oasis of happiness in a desert of five years of childhood misery.

Until the age of six Rudyard Kipling and his three-year-old sister, Trix, had enjoyed a blissful tropical childhood in Bombay complete with doting servants, ayahs and a nursery with the somewhat unorthodox decoration of a stuffed leopard's head. Rudyard's father, John Lockwood Kipling, had sailed to India in 1865 to take up his position as Professor of Architectural Sculpture at the Bombay School of Art, and taken Alice, his young wife, with him. Their first child, Rudyard (named after the lake in Staffordshire where John had proposed to Alice), had been born in Bombay that same year. The young Kipling grew up speaking more Hindustani than English and had to be reminded to speak his mother tongue when with his parents; he was taken to Hindu temples by the family servant Meeta and was read bedtime stories of Indian folk tales. Hardly surprisingly, the smells, sights and sounds of the East were to remain with him for the rest of his life, influencing his work and mood.

Kipling's memory of these idyllic first years was to be a great help during the hard times ahead. These arrived with a vengeance in 1871 after his mother had given birth to her third child who died soon afterwards. No doubt influenced by the death of the baby and the desire to protect their two surviving children from the 'bad air' of India, the Kiplings made the difficult – and expensive – decision to take Ruddy and Trix to the healthier climate of England. Although there were numerous relatives who might have been persuaded to take on the two children, the Kiplings seemed determined not to impose; the two adored and indulged offspring were lodged somewhat questionably in the balmy climes of Southsea near Portsmouth with foster parents found through a newspaper advertisement.

Although Trix, still a toddler with fewer memories of India, was accepted by Captain and Mrs Holloway, the wilful Rudyard was a different matter. Discipline had not formed a major part of his early years; in fact Kipling's Aunt Louisa had written disparagingly after an earlier 'home leave' from her sister that 'Her children turned the house into such a bear-garden, and Ruddy's screaming tempers made Papa so ill, we were thankful to see them on their way. The wretched disturbances one ill-ordered child can make is a lesson for all time to me.'

Mrs Holloway found Kipling's behaviour precocious in the extreme and was determined to break the 'spoilt' child's spirit. With her thirteen-year-old son, Harry, as her accomplice and her hellfire and brimstone brand of Christianity as the driving force, Mrs Holloway undertook her mission. She was astonished that at the age of six, Rudyard could neither read nor write; however, he soon mastered the skill and eagerly pounced on any book in sight – highlighting her own son's slow-wittedness – and was then punished for showing off. Kipling was frequently accused of lying and his punishments varied from learning chunks of the Bible or Book of Common Prayer by heart, being sent to school with a placard bearing the word 'Liar' strapped to his back, being beaten or locked up in the basement or – the worst punishment of all – having his reading material confiscated. This last punishment may well have contributed to his failing eyesight as he resorted to reading books in the dark in secret. By the age of eleven Kipling was half blind and had to wear thick glasses for the rest of his life.

The only respite from the 'House of Desolation', as Kipling was later to call the Holloway's home, was the annual December holiday in Fulham where a month of paradise and love and affection from the Burne-Joneses made some amends for the other eleven months of hell. This house, with the beloved iron bell pull and the gate which 'led to all felicity' was a hub of the pre-Raphaelite and the Arts and Crafts circle and, more importantly, Ruddy's heaven. He recalled the 'most wonderful smells of paint and turpentine whiffing down from the big studio on the first floor where my Uncle worked' and the pleasure of 'the beloved Aunt herself reading us *The Pirate* or *The Arabian Nights* of evenings when one lay out on the big sofas sucking toffee ...'

However, the 'delicious dream' would always end after a month and Kipling would return to the nightmare of Southsea. His rescue was

*A watercolour by Sir Edward Poynter (1836–1919) of Bateman's in
East Sussex where Rudyard Kipling spent much of his life.
(NTPL/Angelo Hornak)*

thanks to his beloved Aunt Georgie who had been alarmed at his failing
sight and depression and wrote to Alice about these worrying develop-
ments. Then in March 1877, as mysteriously as Rudyard's mother had
disappeared from his life six years previously, she reappeared and took
him and Trix away to spend a happy period together before Rudyard
was sent away to public school at the age of twelve, which, compared to
the nightmare of Southsea, could hold no terrors for him. However, the
memories of the House of Desolation were to remain with him for ever
'for when young lips have drunk deep of the bitter waters of Hate,
Suspicion, and Despair, all the love in the world will not wholly take
away that knowledge'.

NOTES

1
Saturday

2
Sunday

'Out of the way, out of the way, there's an angry Ruddy coming!'

Rudyard Kipling as a child

3
Monday

4
Tuesday

5
Wednesday

6
Thursday

7
Friday

8
Saturday

9
Sunday

'Give me the first six years of a child's life and you can have the rest.'

Rudyard Kipling (1865–1936)

10
Monday

11
Tuesday

12
Wednesday

13
Thursday

14
Friday

15
Saturday

16
Sunday

17
Monday

18
Tuesday

19
Wednesday

20
Thursday

21
Friday

22
Saturday

23
Sunday

BRITISH SUMMER TIME ENDS

'Ruddy is a great lark but he won't be a baby much longer. He gets into imminent peril with chairs and things daily. It's the quaintest thing in life to see him eating his supper, intently watched by three dogs.'

Letter from Kipling's father, 1867

24
Monday

25
Tuesday

26
Wednesday

27
Thursday

28
Friday

29
Saturday

30
Sunday

31
Monday

HALLOWE'EN – BANK HOLIDAY (EIRE)

Kipling's empathy with children and his skill at storytelling is recalled by Angela Thirkell, one of the Burne-Jones's grandchildren:

'The *Just So Stories* are a poor thing in print compared with the fun of hearing them told in Cousin Ruddy's deep unhesitating voice. There was a ritual about them, each phrase having its special intonation which had to be exactly the same each time and without which the stories are dried husks. There was an inimitable cadence, an emphasis of certain phrases, a kind of intoning here and there which made his telling unforgettable.'

Rudyard Kipling, Charles Carrington, 1955

NOVEMBER

Small Worlds

Toys and games in the night nursery at Wightwick Manor, West Midlands.
The design of the curtain material, by Charles Voysey,
is used on the cover of this diary.
(NTPL/Andreas von Einsiedel)

Small Worlds

lthough we tend to think of country house nurseries as established elements of the household they are a comparatively recent addition, with their heyday in the Victorian and Edwardian eras. Until the closing decades of the eighteenth century most of the information we have about furnishings for child members of the household is gleaned from contemporary inventories and paintings, giving a tantalising patchwork of individual items rather than an overall view. Records show wealthy families hanging children's beds with luxurious textiles including silk, velvet, gold or silver cloth, oblivious to practical details of damage and cleaning. The main nursery of the newly built Belton House in Lincolnshire is listed in a late seventeenth-century inventory as being furnished with two four-poster beds, one with hangings of crimson mohair, the other curtained in grey angora; the 'little nurserie' meanwhile had a bedstead with purple curtains and a cradle complete with feather mattress and pillows.

However, as the concept of childhood became more accepted, so too was the idea of confining children to the realm of the nursery to spend their time before they were judged ready for entrance into adult society. At the beginning of the nineteenth century the nurseries were usually situated as far away as possible from the social hub of the household: often in the attic. Then, in mid-century, there was a change and many were shifted to be within easy reach of the mother's boudoir and bedroom. This may have been due to the influence of Queen Victoria and Prince Albert who spent many more hours with their children than most Victorian parents; Victoria used to write her journal with Princess Vicky sitting on her lap while Albert amused himself pulling his children round the nursery in a basket. Victoria's complaint of the Buckingham Palace nursery wing was that it was 'literally a mile off' making impromptu visits logistically impossible. This fault was corrected at their Isle of Wight holiday residence, Osborne House, which was designed with a family wing where the royal parents simply had to climb one flight of stairs to the floor above to see their children – infinitely preferable to the hike along Buckingham Palace's corridors. Other country house owners followed suit. After a disastrous fire in 1881, Lanhydrock in Cornwall was rebuilt with a nursery on the first floor which was completely self-sufficient but nevertheless within reach of Lord and Lady Robartes' private rooms.

Once the nursery had been accepted as a domain in its own right the question of décor inevitably arose, and the last decades of the nineteenth century witnessed the flowering of nursery art. Eager parents flocked to luxury stores, such as Liberty, Heal's and the Army and Navy, which had begun to stock tiles, wallpapers and all the other essentials for the well-equipped and fashionable nursery.

Walter Crane, a disciple of William Morris, and, among other things, the Principal of the Royal College of Art and President of the Art Workers' Guild, was one of the first artists to concentrate on nursery furnishings. His beautifully illustrated children's books had already been a success but unlike many of the artists later to be connected with nursery furnishings, such as Kate Greenaway, Crane designed specifically for wallpaper rather than simply selling the reproduction rights of existing book illustrations to manufacturers to be adapted for wall coverings. Between 1875 and 1906 Jeffrey & Co printed seven Crane-designed wallpapers for the public and one exclusive design for the nursery of Castle Howard in Yorkshire.

In the early decades of the twentieth century other top designers turned their minds to all aspects of nursery design. Charles Voysey produced a delightful design for curtains called *The House that Jack Built* which now hangs from the nursery windows of Wightwick Manor, West Midlands (see diary cover). Charles Rennie Mackintosh designed a nursery in Art Nouveau style. Richard Norman Shaw conceived a delightful cot in the Arts and Crafts manner, complete with a medieval-style starred hood, while the exterior featured an eclectic subject range of painted panels including the signs of the Zodiac. Even Edwin Lutyens made a concession to the nursery vogue by incorporating a window at toddler height in the nursery of Castle Drogo, Julius Drewe's modern castle in Devon.

Along with the craze for wallpapers came the fashion for decorated crockery for nursery teas. Children's china was, in fact, the forerunner of commemorative mugs for royal events and momentous national occasions. Small charges were urged to eat off plates commemorating such diverse subjects as the 'Opening of the Thames Tunnel between Rotherhithe and Wapping' or the death of Sir Robert Peel. When

*An early eighteenth-century portrait of Gerard Anne Edwards (1732–73)
by William Hogarth from the Bearsted Collection at Upton House,
Warwickshire. The baby is shown sitting in a wicker cradle draped with yards
of quilted fabric. (NTPL/Angelo Hornak)*

children were not being spoon-fed from dishes bearing dull or morbid subjects they were being inflicted with plates festooned with Victorian sentimentality. With subjects like these there can have been little incentive to eat up and reveal the pattern decorating the bottom of the plate.

However, towards the end of the nineteenth century favourite characters from nursery books began to appear on dishes and cups – and the idea of merchandising was born. Kate Greenaway's designs were some of the first to be used and they were soon followed by Mabel Lucie Attwell's distinctive characters. Yet the most popular designs belonged to that perennial favourite – the cuddly bunny in assorted guises. Royal Doulton produced the Bunnykins range in 1925 while Beatrix Potter's creations, Peter Rabbit and Benjamin Bunny, proved ideal subjects for chinaware and are still hopping around the rims of Wedgwood nursery plates and mugs today. Feeding time had become fun – especially if you liked rabbits.

1
Tuesday

2
Wednesday

3
Thursday

4
Friday

5
Saturday

GUY FAWKES' NIGHT

6
Sunday

'The nursery is a place where the children can enjoy a full measure of peace without their lives being disturbed by the activities of the grown-ups.'

The English House, Herman Muthesius, 1904

7
Monday

8
Tuesday

9
Wednesday

10
Thursday

11
Friday

12
Saturday

13
Sunday

REMEMBRANCE SUNDAY

A 1683 inventory for Ham House in Surrey records 'two chayres for children the one black and the other japanned'. Nearly two hundred years later an inventory for Speke Hall in Merseyside lists a carved, ebonised oak chair upholstered in red leather made for the four-year-old daughter of the house, Adelaide Watt, to match the adult suite: it was 29 inches high as opposed to the adult version of 47 inches.

14
Monday

15
Tuesday

16
Wednesday

17
Thursday

18
Friday

19
Saturday

20
Sunday

21
Monday

22
Tuesday

23
Wednesday

24
Thursday

25
Friday

26
Saturday

27
Sunday

FIRST SUNDAY IN ADVENT

Ellen Terry, the renowned Victorian actress who lived at Smallhythe Place in Kent, recalled that her children 'were allowed no rubbishy books, but from the first, Japanese prints lined the walls and Walter Crane was their classic.'

28
Monday

29
Tuesday

30
Wednesday

ST ANDREW'S DAY

'We could never have loved earth so well if we had had no childhood in it.'

George Eliot (1819–80)

DECEMBER

The Magic of Christmas

Charles Wade who lived at Snowshill Manor in Gloucestershire recalled magical Christmases of his childhood in this drawing of presents under the tree.
(NTPL/Ray Hallett)

The Magic of Christmas

There might, if this weather held, be skating or better still tobogganing, for which the slopes of the park were so well suited – but the weather did not matter. How could it, with a house full of delightful visitors and such a house to play in? There would be the Christmas tree with all its presents; games in the drawing rooms, music and dancing in the hall, private theatricals in the Long Gallery; hide-and-seek all over the house, with people chasing each other in delicious terror the whole length of the long corridors; wonderful meals in the dining room, dinners as well as luncheons even for little girls, and all the time everybody, particularly the grown-ups, happy, good-humoured, joking and jolly, ready at any moment to romp and play the fool.

hyllis Sandeman, the youngest daughter of Lord and Lady Newton, grew up at Lyme Park in Cheshire at the turn of the century, with her four brothers and sisters. Her memories of these halcyon childhood days are captured in her book *Treasure on Earth* and revolve around her recollections of the activities leading up to and following Christmas.

Many of the festive practices had their origins in more ancient medieval rites when feasting would have continued over the whole two-week period from Christmas Eve to Epiphany. During this time the Lord of the Manor would show great largess to his house-guests and on at least one day would throw open his doors (and kitchens) to anyone who happened to pass by. This could result in banquets of huge proportions for relative strangers. In 1507 the Duke of Buckingham found himself with 182 'strangers' at his Christmas Day dinner, and the number was to increase to 319 guests at Epiphany. Elaborate food would grace the tables – stuffed boars' heads and game birds of all descriptions – all consumed to the sound of minstrels playing in the gallery. Left-overs from the meal would be distributed to the beggars at the gate. After eating, the tables would be cleared to make way for the arrival of the mummers.

Hundreds of years later, at Lyme Park, the run-up to Christmas was slightly more restrained but still a period of great celebration and

Painted in 1891 by Viggo Johansen (1851–1935), Happy Christmas *depicts children dancing round a tree laden with presents, crackers, decorations and lighted candles. (Hirsch Sprungske Collection, Copenhagen/Bridgeman Art Library)*

ritual. Whereas medieval great halls would have been decked with holly and other evergreens, from the pagan belief that they scared away evil spirits, Lyme Park followed the relatively new fashion brought to England by Prince Albert from his native Germany, with a decorated fir tree in the Long Gallery. Phyllis recalls the thrill of seeing the decorated tree for the first time:

'There were rainbow-coloured, iridescent glass balls hanging singly and in garlands, showers of sparkling tinsel, spun glass humming birds, bells and stars, trumpets and violins, small toy crocodiles and golliwogs, a figure of Father Christmas on the topmost branch and, of course, innumerable candles.'

The Long Gallery was also the scene for the amateur theatricals – as integral a part of Christmas celebrations as mummers in times past. The Lyme estate carpenter was commissioned to build the stage and scenery in time for rehearsals to start on Boxing Day, although the first day of rehearsing was always hindered slightly by the absence of most of the male actors on the traditional Boxing Day shoot. The organisation of the play was one of Phyllis's strongest memories as the children were given substantial parts, taking their roles extremely seriously. Part of the undoubted thrill of Christmas for the children of the house was this opportunity of mingling with adult society – whether it was participating in the play or being allowed to eat off the silver plate in the grand dining-room and sip champagne from crystal glasses instead of being confined to the nursery with their governess. The excitement also lay in seeing adults behave like children for a change. Phyllis's Aunt Lucy was a case in point: 'She suddenly threw herself back in her chair, waved her legs in the air and cried: "Hurrah! Christmas Day to-morrow."'

Her father, however, was not one to succumb too easily to the festive spirit, particularly during Christmas dinner: 'With dessert came the crackers, always a trial to Sir Thomas [Lord Newton], for whom the sight of grown men and women in paper caps was anathema.'

Christmas was also a period, as in the past, to show hospitality and kindness to employees and the Lyme estate was no exception. As the lady of the house, Phyllis's mother was responsible for distributing gifts to the estate workers. The first of these ceremonies took place in the kitchens on Christmas Eve:

'One after another, each man employed on the estate entered, advanced to the table and spread out a huge cotton handkerchief, the shepherd dumped a joint of beef upon it and Lady Vayne [Lady Newton], gathering up the corners, just, but only just, succeeded in knotting them over the joint. Having done this, she wished the recipient a happy Christmas and received his good wishes in return.'

The high point of festivities – for servants and guests alike – was the Servants' Ball which took place in the Hall on New Year's Eve. Each servant was allowed to bring a guest and dancing continued well into the early hours of the morning, with some housemaids foregoing sleep in order to make the most of the party. The Servants' Ball at Lyme was unusual in that it took place above stairs and was attended by both servants and all the members of the house party, children included, although integration was not encouraged off the dance floor: 'The house party was expected to keep to their end of the room during dances'.

The splendour of Christmas celebrations, such as those at Lyme, have probably gone for ever, but the emotions and excitement felt by Phyllis are shared by every child who gazes longingly at the presents under their own tree, or rips open their stocking on Christmas morning.

1
Thursday

2
Friday

3
Saturday

4
Sunday

'Early awake in the darkness before Nurse had time to draw the curtains, full of eager expectancy, we crept to the bed post over the billowy eiderdown to feel the exciting bulges in the stocking. Then, when at last dawned the day, what cries of delight and glee as we unwrapped the many toys that our stockings contained, delving down to the toe which produced a fine glowing orange. What an exciting pile of treasures lay on the eiderdown amidst the whisps of crumpled coloured paper.'

Days Far Away, Charles Wade (1883–1956)

5
Monday

6
Tuesday

7
Wednesday

8
Thursday

9
Friday

10
Saturday

11
Sunday

'And girls in slacks remember Dad,
And oafish louts remember Mum,
And sleepless children's hearts are glad
And Christmas-morning bells say 'Come!'
Even to shining ones who dwell
Safe in the Dorchester Hotel.'

Few Late Chrysanthemums, Christmas, Sir John Betjeman (1906–84)

12
Monday

13
Tuesday

14
Wednesday

15
Thursday

16
Friday

17
Saturday

18
Sunday

19
Monday

20
Tuesday

21
Wednesday

THE SHORTEST DAY

22
Thursday

23
Friday

24
Saturday

CHRISTMAS EVE

25
Sunday

CHRISTMAS DAY

'God bless the master of this house,
The mistress also,
And all the little children,
That round the table go.
And all your kin and kinsmen
That dwell both near and far,
I wish you a Merry Christmas
And a Happy New Year.'

Traditional carol

DECEMBER

26
Monday

BOXING DAY (UK)

27
Tuesday

BANK HOLIDAY (UK)

28
Wednesday

29
Thursday

30
Friday

31
Saturday

'Parents are the last people on earth who ought to have children.'

Samuel Butler (1612–80)

NOTES

NOTES

NOTES